I0423158

IDEAS FOR $AVING AMERICA

— *Start in 2012* —

BY CARTER COBERLY

PREFACE

The reason for this book is my worry about the future of America. I am not concerned for myself, but for my children and grandchildren. America has been the land of opportunity for many generations of my family and me. America provided me with unlimited opportunities and freedoms to succeed and to fail. The American government, established by our Founding Fathers, is the best government the world has ever known. It was an experiment which proved to be wildly successful, at least until now.

I am retired and an early part of the baby-boom generation. My generation made incredible progress in knowledge, technology, science, arts, entertainment, religion, and much more. We have raised the standard of living and made life easier for almost everyone. Unfortunately, we may also be the generation who will destroy America. There are radical elements in my generation who seem to hate the America of the past and are working hard to remake it. They view the American government created by our Founding Fathers as quaint, but out of touch for today. They believe that they have much better ideas on how the government should operate and have imposed their ideas on us over the past 50 years. The results of their changes are vividly seen today and are having major impacts on all of our lives. The America of yesteryear is almost gone, along with the opportunities, freedoms, and liberties.

The purpose of this book is to help save America. My life is nearing its end, so maybe I shouldn't care. I will be moving on to a new spiritual life with God. But I do care about the lives of my children and grandchildren. Therefore, I feel compelled to help. I have to try and stop the radical, delusional, drug-induced, and self-centered part of my generation from destroying the best country and government on earth. I would like for the baby-boom generation to be remembered for all of its incredibly positive accomplishments. However, those will be quickly forgotten if we allow the radicals of my generation to destroy America.

I am sure that the radicals truly believe in what they are doing. Through a very powerful centralized government, they will be able to control all aspects of American lives and will be able to create a utopia here on earth. In their minds, every

American will be equal and will equally share in the bounty. All we have to do is comply with their wishes and every demand. They will plan and control it all for us. Through their efforts, we will be healthy, happy, well-fed, clothed, and able to live a better life. However, there may be a few things which we will need to give up. Our Christian faith will no longer be needed or tolerated. Marriage between a man and woman will be an ancient concept. We will spend many hours of our day recycling and watching propaganda entertainment on TV. Our guns and weapons of any kind will be confiscated. Our houses or apartments will be limited in size, color choices, plants allowed, roof types, heat sources, insulation amounts, maximum window area, and must be located within highly dense cities. Since radicals hate the internal combustion engine, private automobiles and living in the country will be outlawed, even for farmers. Travel to and from work, school, and retail shops will only be allowed using public transportation. Our number of children will be limited to one and that is only if we are selected via a child lottery. The child lottery may be rigged to ensure that undesirable parents are not selected. Steps will be taken to ensure reproduction will not occur when it is not authorized by the controlling elite. It is difficult to imagine all the new laws and restrictions which will be imposed. Many of the new laws described have already been implemented in socialist societies, in specific locales within the U.S., and/or discussed by various leaders of the liberal fringe. However, none of these laws and restrictions will apply to the elite in charge.

This is not the America which I want for my children and grandchildren. I love them too much for that. Join me in standing up against the baby-boom radicals and all the revolutionary groups who have joined them. Mob violence is already underway in many parts of the world and will likely spread to the U.S. in the near future. The mob leaders' primary goal will be to overthrow the current U.S. government and replace it with a socialist one. The baby-boom radicals have made huge progress towards a socialist government in the U.S., but are becoming impatient. They want to accomplish the goal before their lives end. Let's stop them now before it is too late for America. I prefer the American government in which I was raised. I prefer a government of opportunity, freedom, and liberty for my children and grandchildren, not an elitist socialist government where freedom and liberty are only a memory and the government controls every aspect of life. As Thomas Jefferson said, "My reading of history convinces me that most bad government results from too much government."

CHAPTER 1:

CHANGE THE TAX STRUCTURE

The first and most important idea for saving America is to eliminate the **federal, state, and city income taxes** in the U.S. for individuals and corporations. Many ideas which follow in this book are dependent upon enactment of this first critical idea.

Federal income taxes were established and started in 1913 with the 16th Amendment to the U. S. Constitution. This amendment was sold to the American people and state legislators as a tax on the super-rich only, never to touch the middle and lower classes. Originally, the income tax ranged from 1% to 7% of net income. In other words, the amendment's approval was based on misinformation. If the American people had been told the truth, how this income tax would be expanded to virtually everyone and the percentages increased to incredibly high levels (above 90%), the amendment would never have been ratified. It is time to repeal an amendment which was passed either upon misinformation or outright deception.

In the State of Washington, a state income tax is considered unconstitutional based upon the state's constitution. For years, initiatives have been submitted to the citizens of Washington State to authorize a state income tax. Each initiative has been voted down by a large majority of the state's residents. The primary reason is that the residents of Washington State do not trust their politicians to limit this income tax to only the rich and to a small percentage of income. The citizens have learned from history and do not want it repeated in their state. They know that once a state income tax is implemented, it will be increased continuously and to levels beyond anything imagined.

Income taxes are expensive to collect. Income tax rules are complex. There are thousands of pages of instructions and virtually no one understands them all. There are endless hours of accounting required to track wages, business incomes, and deductible expenses. There is a myriad of methods for hiding special tax deductions within the tax code which only apply to a specific person, company, or industry. The opportunity for tax abuse is enormous. Is there anyone in the U.S. who thinks that the income tax is applied fairly or that everyone pays their fair share?

Income taxes keep small start-up businesses from being successful. Many individual entrepreneurs have unique skills and ideas which lend themselves to starting small businesses. These U.S. citizens attempt to operate their small businesses on a part-time or full-time basis. A large percentage of these businesses fail because of the overhead expenses which are associated with record keeping and paperwork which must be filed with the IRS. The overhead costs associated with income taxes drain the limited profits of these businesses in their early life and thus cause the entrepreneurs to shut down the businesses before they become more profitable. Many of these businesses would be successful if income taxes were not required.

Income taxes are prone to fraud and abuse. People hide income made from their home businesses. Some people deal only in cash so transactions cannot be traced. The illegal drug trade is a good example of large incomes which go unreported. Taxpayers embellish expenses and deductions by claiming larger amounts than actually paid. They are playing the odds that they will not be audited by the IRS. Special exemptions are passed by Congress which reduce taxes for a few rich friends or companies who have provided large campaign contributions. This adds to the complexity of the tax code. Also, the income taxes paid by individuals are considered private information, not public information, thus making fraud more attractive and easier to hide. No one will know that some taxpayers are paying less than required. This makes it hard for citizens to expose cheaters.

If the federal income tax is abolished, the state and city income taxes must also be abolished. If the state and city income taxes were to continue, the costs to comply with income taxes would still be imposed and thus the overhead costs would still be required. The revenue lost by the federal, state, and local governments could be replaced with alternative taxes and tax rate increases.

Income taxes on both individuals and corporations are a drag on the U.S. economy. The income tax rate on corporations is 39%, whereas the corporate income tax rate in many other countries is much less. Corporations can move their operations to countries offering lower taxes and regulations, thus avoid paying the higher U.S. income taxes. This is happening at record levels. If the U.S. corporate income tax was eliminated, many corporations would move their operations back to the U.S. because it would make financial sense. Individuals can move their funds into some offshore bank accounts and avoid paying U.S. income taxes. Large surpluses of individual and corporate funds remain outside the U.S. today because of the income taxes which will be imposed if the funds are returned.

This reduces capital available for starting new businesses within the U.S.

If individual and corporate income taxes are repealed, there will be a resurgence of productive jobs created in the U.S. The disincentive created by income taxes on productive work will be eliminated. Small businesses will be able to focus completely on expanding their products and services with no distractions related to IRS paperwork, forms, or reporting. Their overhead costs will be reduced significantly and their profits increased. Entrepreneurs will make decisions for improving or growing their products or services rather than minimizing their income tax liabilities.

If the U.S. repealed income taxes at the federal, state, and local levels, where will these governments get the revenue they need for their operation? That question is answered in the following sections.

Replace the federal, state, and local income taxes with the following three new taxes.

1) **Federal wealth tax**. A federal wealth tax is a tax on the assets of America, its people, corporations, partnerships, trusts, or any legal entity who owns wealth. Only those who own assets will need to pay taxes. The wealth tax should apply to assets of $5,000 or greater which are contained within the U.S. and its territories or owned by U.S. citi-

zens, corporations, partnerships, trusts, or any legal entity who owns assets. The $5,000 amount was chosen as the minimum taxable value in order to eliminate taxing the many inexpensive assets that Americans own, but to make sure that most voting Americans will be taxed at some level because most voters will have assets of $5,000 or greater. If tax rates are raised or lowered by the federal government, everyone should feel the pain or benefit of those rate changes.

Taxable assets will include land, underground resources, above-the-ground resources, structures, buildings, vehicles, stocks, bonds, bank accounts, cash, commodities, jewelry, paintings, livestock, and other assets. **Land** will include undeveloped properties, farms, lots, privately owned timber, railroad properties, privately owned toll roads, and any other non-government owned properties within the U.S. or its territories. **Underground resources** include known reserves of oil, natural gas, coal, gold, silver, uranium, copper, aluminum, and other like natural resources. **Above-the-ground** resources include gold, silver, uranium, copper, aluminum, oil, natural gas, coal, uranium or other like resources. **Structures and buildings** include houses, office buildings, skyscrapers, utility buildings, power generating windmills, billboards, factories, and other like structures and buildings. **Vehicles** include automobiles, trucks, farm equipment, construction equipment, boats, ships, trains, airplanes, motorcycles, and other like vehicles. **Stocks and bonds** will be based on the end-of-year values of all stocks and bonds owned, including those contained in mutual funds and like financial funds. The $5,000 or greater limit will apply to the total value of stocks and bonds, not each individual stock or bond. The total will include the value of both U.S. and foreign owned stocks and bonds. **Bank accounts** will be based on the end-of-year cash balances of U.S. citizens. This will include cash balances within both U.S. and foreign banks. **Cash** will be based upon the end-of-year total amount of $5,000 or greater contained within the U.S. and foreign locations. **Commodities** will be based upon the total value owned of corn, soybeans, wheat, cotton, coffee, bananas, pineapple, or any other like commodities which are $5,000 or greater. **Jewelry and paintings** will include each individual item which has a value of $5,000 or greater. **Livestock** will be based upon the total value of horses, cows, sheep, pigs, chickens, or other animals where the $5,000 limit is based on the total owned, not each individual horse, cow, sheep, pig, or chicken. **Other assets** include any asset which has an individual value of $5,000 or greater.

The total value of all assets within the U.S. and its territories is unknown at present, but a total value of $100 trillion will be used as an estimate. With a federal budget of $2 trillion, not counting Social Security, federal retirement, Medicare, Medicaid, and interest on the debt, which will be discussed later in this book, the yearly tax rate percentage on all assets will be 2%. Therefore, the federal wealth tax on a $150,000 house will be $3,000. The wealth tax on a $30,000 car will be $600. The federal wealth tax will replace the federal income tax. As an alternative to the flat 2% tax rate, the tax rate percentage could be graduated, such that the percentage paid is increased as the total wealth per individual is increased. For example, a 1% rate could be charged for individual and corporate assets up to $1 million, 2% rate from $1 million to $10 million, and 3% rate above $10 million. These different rates will need to be determined and based on the total federal government revenue needed, the total calculated U.S. wealth, and the distribution of that wealth. As the wealth of the nation increases and the costs of the federal government are reduced, the wealth tax percentage should be reduced over time with the goal of a 1% tax rate.

The top 1% of households in America own 38% of the wealth, the top 3.5% own about 50% of the wealth, and the top 10% own 71%. Since rich individuals, corporations, partnerships, trusts, and, in some instances, foreigners, own a large percentage of property and wealth in the U.S. and its territories, this approach will tax those who can best afford it. All taxes will come from people with wealth above $5,000.

The changes in total wealth value each year will be small and will likely increase, thus making the next year's tax revenue prediction very accurate, stable, and growing.

Wealth taxes should be much less expensive to collect. The current costs for collecting property tax are significantly less than for collecting income taxes since most property remains the same for years. With the income tax abolished, the IRS can be used to assess wealth values each year and collect the taxes due. The IRS can be retrained to determine wealth values throughout the U.S. and its territories and to track the owners of this wealth. If the taxes will not, or cannot, be paid, liens can be placed on the wealth, if it is property, and the property can be sold for the taxes. Farmers can protect their farms by purchasing crop insurance which will replace income lost from crop failures due to drought and other natural causes.

Wealth taxes for property should be public information. Therefore, it will be difficult to hide wealth in order to avoid the wealth taxes. Any citizen will be able to evaluate the wealth taxes paid by others and help determine if someone, for some reason, is hiding assets or underpaying on existing assets. This will help make taxes fairer and more difficult for special interests to get special tax breaks without the public knowing. This will hopefully lead to a dis-incentive for special interest groups and individuals who make large political campaign contributions, since the benefits in doing so are reduced.

2) **Federal wealth-increase tax**. A second proposed tax to replace the federal income tax is a wealth-in-crease tax. This is a tax on the *increase* in the wealth of individuals, trusts, corporations, and partner-ships when it is $1 million per year or more. This is not an income tax but a tax on the increase in wealth. Wealth will include the total increase in value of stocks, bonds, interest earned, dividends received, value of worldwide bank accounts, value of precious metals, etc.

Currently, billionaires, like Warren Buffet and Bill Gates, do not pay taxes on their billions in wealth increase because their wealth is held in in-vestments which they rarely sell. For example, if they own stocks which increase by $100 million in a year, they pay nothing for that increase in wealth if they don't sell the stocks. They aren't taxed unless they sell, which will likely never happen. Instead, their wealth will be put into very large trust funds and given to the charities of their choice. Shouldn't some of these billions be taxed? Using their ap-proach, the tax code allows 100% deduction for their charitable giving.

The tax rate for the wealth-increase tax should have a maximum percentage limit, such as 15%.

Taxing a wealth increase of $1 million or more will have a much less negative impact on the U.S. economy than taxing income as done today. Taxing wealth will not create a disincentive for maximizing income. Taxes are only applied once the income is added to a person's wealth and that increase exceeds $1 million. In addition, the wealth-increase tax rate percentage will be less than the tax rates which are now applied to income.

3) **Federal one-time wealth-increase tax**. A third proposed tax to replace the federal income tax is a one-time wealth-increase tax. This is a tax which will only be assessed once, when the tax laws are changed from a federal income tax to the wealth tax and wealth-increase tax. It will be a tax on wealth of over $1 million, accumulated by individuals, trusts, partnerships, and corporations who haven't already been charged income taxes for that wealth in the past 30 years.

Again, Warren Buffet and Bill Gates are used as examples. They should pay a one-time tax on all their accumulated wealth for which no income taxes have been paid up to the new tax kick-off date. Also, taxes should be charged on the amounts already given to charities. They should not be allowed to take 100% deductions of their wealth increase by giving it to the charities of their choice. The average American is not allowed this luxury.

Requiring payment immediately for the total taxes due for this one-time wealth-increase tax may create a hardship for those who owe. Therefore, allow the one-time wealth-increase tax to be paid over a period of 10 years, but charge 5% interest on the unpaid balance. Also, apply liens against the wealth to ensure that the taxes will be collected.

One hundred percent of the one-time wealth-increase taxes should be used to help replenish the Social Security trust fund which will be discussed later in this book. The tax rate should have a maximum percentage limit, such as 15%.

When the tax laws are changed from an income tax to the three new taxes discussed above, include a provision in law which will restrict the federal government from spending more than is collected in taxes. In other words, do not allow deficit spending. The Congress should set the tax rate percentages for the coming year based upon the federal budget they pass and the forecasted tax revenue. Since the tax revenue will be estimated, the tax rates should be set high enough to ensure that the revenue collected will pay for next year's budget. Revenue collected above the yearly budget can be used to help reduce taxes the following year.

The following is an example of how the proposed tax changes will affect two people, Bob Billionaire and Joe Average.

Bob Billionaire and his wife are in their sixties and have two grown children. Joe Average and his wife are in their thirties and have two children in grade school.

Bob is the owner and manager of his own privately held business which provides products which are in demand in the U.S. and throughout the world. This last year, the business had revenue of $250 million and provided a net profit of $25 million. The actual net cash received by Bob was $100 million but Bob's tax accountants and lawyers were able to reduce his taxable income to $25 million by using legal deductions and credits, such as depreciation, depletion allowances, charitable giving, foreign tax credits, and special income tax deductions for his business. Bob's business has been very successful for many years and Bob has accumulated much wealth over those years. He has purchased many properties, stocks, bonds, and other investments which have gone up significantly in value over the years. Bob rarely sells any of his properties, stocks, bonds, or other investments and, hence, does not pay any income taxes on their increased values. Bob's business is set up as a corporation and the business paid *corporate income taxes on the net $25 million at 39%, or $9.75 million. Bob paid himself a yearly salary of $1 million from the business so his personal tax was about $0.25 million including his Social Security and Medicare taxes. Therefore, Bob's total income tax for himself and the business was $10 million.*

Bob's wealth has grown over the years to about $1 billion. His wealth is from retained earnings from his business as well as the growth in value of his investments. The following table provides a breakdown of his wealth.

BOB BILLIONAIRE'S ASSETS	VALUE (in millions)
Primary residence	$10
Worldwide vacation homes	$25
Investment land (10,000 acres)	$50
Business office buildings	$25
Stocks, U.S. and foreign	$500
Bonds, tax exempt municipal	$200
Vehicles, including private plane	$25
Cash is U.S. banks	$20
Cash in foreign banks	$50
Jewelry and paintings	$20
Gold and silver	$75
TOTAL	$1,000

What will Bob's taxes be for the three wealth taxes proposed? 1) Assuming a 2% wealth tax rate, Bob's wealth tax on his $1 billion will be $20 million. 2) Bob's increase in wealth for the year is $100 million, the net cash increase he received. If the wealth-increase tax percentage is set at 15%, Bob will owe an additional $15 *million. 3) It is estimated that $200 million of Bob's total wealth is from increased values of the properties, stocks, jewelry, paintings, gold, and silver for which no taxes have ever been paid for the increase in value. If the one-time wealth-increase tax rate is set at 15%, Bob will owe another $30 million in taxes for the first year in which the federal income taxes are changed to the wealth taxes. Bob will be allowed 10 years to pay this $30 million, or $3 million per year. Based on this hypothetical example, Bob's total wealth taxes would be $38 million for this year versus $10 million for income taxes. Bob will not like paying the higher taxes, but can well afford it. At $38 million, the tax percentage based on his total wealth is 3.8%. In this example, Bob's wealth increased by $100 million from his business. Assuming an average 5% rate of return on his investments, his wealth also increased by $50 million from his investments. Thus, his total federal taxes are 25% of his total wealth increase of $150 million. Bob's business, properties, investments, and other assets benefit from the services provided by the federal government, such as military protection, transportation systems, legal protection, patent protection, international trade agreements, private property rights, etc. Therefore, Bob needs to pay his fair share of the expenses for these services.*

Joe Average and his wife both work full time in order to pay the family living expenses. Together, they make $50,000 per year of income. They own a modest house valued at $150,000. They also own two older cars since they work in different areas and their work hours don't allow them to commute together. The cars are valued at $10,000 each. They haven't been able to save much, so they have less than $5,000 in their joint bank account. They have been able to put retirement money into their 401K plans at their companies and the total value is currently $30,000. They have no other assets with a value of $5,000 or greater.

The federal income taxes paid by Joe and his wife are about 6% of their income, or $3,000 per year. They and their companies also pay another $7,000 in taxes for Social Security and Medicare. The funds paid into these federal programs are considered taxes in this example since there is no guarantee that Joe and his wife will ever receive any benefits. Under the current federal income tax system, Joe and his wife paid a total of $10,000 or 20% of their income to the federal government. Bob Billionaire paid $10 million of $150 million in real wealth increase, or only 6.7%. Bob should be paying the same or higher percentage than Joe, but under the current tax system pays less.

If the income tax were replaced with the wealth taxes proposed, Joe and his wife will pay 2% of *their wealth in taxes. The taxes will be applied to their $150,000 house, two $10,000 cars, and $30,000 invested in the 401K plans for a total of $200,000. Therefore, their federal wealth tax will be $4,000 per year. In later chapters, changes to Social Security and Medicare are discussed, which will eliminate them as **taxes** to Joe and his wife. Since Joe's wealth is less than $1 million, the wealth-increase and one-time wealth-increase taxes are zero. The total federal taxes paid by Joe and his wife are 2% of wealth, or 8% of wages, compared to 3.8% of wealth, or 25% of wealth increase for Bob Billionaire. The tax percentages are fairer using the wealth tax method than the income tax method. If a graduated wealth tax rate is applied of 1% for wealth less than $1 million, Joe's taxes would be decreased in half to $2,000. If the wealth tax is increased from 2% to 3% for wealth over $10 million, Bob Billionaire's taxes will be increased by $10 million.*

Hopefully, this fictitious comparison helps in understanding the tax changes proposed. Wealthy individuals will pay more in taxes, but their costs for complying with the complex income tax rules will be reduced. There will also be no disincentive for growing their businesses to maximize income. Their growth in wealth each year will be faster using the wealth tax system rather than the income tax system. This additional growth will likely pay a large percentage of the higher wealth taxes. The federal revenue will be increased to the level needed to fund the government, thus eliminating budget deficits. And the federal wealth tax collected will be consistent year after year, since the country's wealth will not change drastically each year.

As a side note, the federal government should eliminate the myriad of other current federal taxes, such as telephone tax, inheritance tax, gasoline tax, airline tax, etc. The funding of the federal government should be limited to the federal wealth tax, wealth-increase tax, and one-time wealth-increase tax. It should be clear to U.S. citizens what they are paying in total federal taxes. Citizens distrust the government when they appear to spread federal taxes across multiple products and services for the purpose of hiding the total taxes being paid.

4) **State sales tax**. The taxes collected by state governments should be limited to a sales tax, eliminating the state income taxes. Each state should set the sales tax rate to a percentage which would meet their yearly budget needs. The states should eliminate other taxes and fees, including motel taxes, car license fees, special fuel taxes, etc. The sales tax collected on car sales should cover the car license. Likewise, the sales tax collected for fuel should be the same as for any other product. Most fuel is con-

sumed for productive purposes, including hauling goods, commuting, and shopping. All of these activities are beneficial to the state and its citizens.

As an alternative to the sales tax, a state may want to collect their taxes by adding a percentage to the wealth taxes proposed, which will be charged to the residents of their state instead of collecting a sales tax. Each state can decide what works best for them.

5) **Local taxes**. Local governments currently charge **property taxes** to meet their budget needs. They should either continue to collect property taxes, if desired, or possibly switch to the federal government's wealth tax and collect their taxes with a local percentage added to the wealth tax of the citizens who live in the community. Switching to the wealth tax will help them lower the tax rate percentages that they currently charge. City and county governments should replace income taxes with either additional sales taxes or wealth taxes. Allow other specific income needs, like unemployment insurance, to be handled as they are today.

U.S. taxes need to be simplified and government budgets need to be balanced. This will allow the country to prosper by creating a stable business environment. Non-productive paperwork will be eliminated and people can concentrate on providing goods and services needed within a stable, non-inflationary country.

CHAPTER 2:

SOCIAL SECURITY

Today, the Social Security program is in trouble because of the mismanagement and raiding of funds by Congress over the last 50 years. All the payroll taxes paid into Social Security have been used by Congress as just another source of income to pay for ever-increasing federal government programs and spending. Those who are retired or nearing retirement will now need to rely on the payroll taxes of their children and grandchildren. Their children and grandchildren believe that they will never receive a dime from Social Security for their retirements. Because Congress has spent all of the citizens' savings paid into Social Security, it has become a Ponzi scheme, where payments are made to current retirees from the payroll taxes collected from those still working.

In addition, Congress has expanded the scope of Social Security, making it a new federal government welfare program. Supplemental Social Security is now paid to millions of Americans under retirement age, for various disabilities. Young adults in their 20's are collecting monthly checks for disabilities, such as alcoholism, severe depression, back pain, etc. State governments have been working hard over the past decade to remove people from their welfare rolls, which are funded by the states, and help them qualify for Supplemental Social Security which is funded by the federal government. The costs for Supplemental Social Security are rising faster than retirement costs.

Social Security is not sustainable as is without significant increases in payroll taxes on our children and grandchildren. The taxes will eventually reach a level where the children and grandchildren will refuse to pay and the program will be scrapped. Major changes are needed now if the program is to be saved.

In the past, and even today, Social Security payroll taxes are mixed with other federal taxes collected, thus increasing the total funds that the federal government spends. In the past, when more Social Security funds were collected than spent, this provided a windfall of money that was spent on the politicians' favorite programs. The result was that no Social Security funds were saved and invested so that the funds could grow and earn interest. Instead, the funds allowed the federal government to grow their spending beyond limits that anyone could imagine. This led to even more federal government spending using deficits. The result is the massive liability which we now have and no savings to pay for retirements. The following story provides a simple analogy of what happened and where we are.

This story is about a husband, wife, and their two children. In order to be gender neutral, the terms spouse1 and spouse2 will be used rather than the terms husband and wife, not identifying which is which.

Spouse1 and spouse2 agree that they should take a portion of their income each year and put it away for retirement. Spouse1 and spouse2 each plan to retire at age 65. They agree that 6% of their yearly funds should go into savings, which will be used for retirement. Since this family makes the average American income of $50,000 per year (ignoring the distorting effects of government caused inflation), their average savings is $3,000 per year. They save starting with their first jobs and both spouse1 and spouse2 are able to work for 45 years each (age 20 to 65). The money put into savings will be $3,000 per year times 45 years, or $135,000. During those 45 years, the money will be put into conservative investments which earn an average of 5% per year. Therefore, the value of their savings at retirement will be approximately $480,000. At retirement, the couple wants to withdraw $50,000 per year in order to live at the same level as when they were working. However, at that withdrawal rate, the retirement funds will only last about 13 years, assuming a continuing interest is paid of 5% on the remaining balance. When the couple realizes that the funds will only last until they reach age 78, they decide to reduce the withdrawal rate so the funds will last until they are at least 85 (20 years). Therefore, they plan to reduce the yearly payout at retirement, knowing they will have reduced expenses associated with work, such as buying lunches, commuting, work clothing, etc. They calculate that $38,000 per year can be withdrawn and last them over 20 years. So they agree on this plan and execute it faithfully. Well, that isn't exactly what happened.

Spouse1 controlled the retirement savings account and did not let spouse2 ever look at the balance. The reason given was that a large balance in the account might tempt spouse2 to want to withdraw the funds in order to pay for an "emergency" or something frivolous. So, spouse1 always tells spouse2 that the savings "trust fund" is adequately funded to pay for their retirement. What spouse2 didn't know was that once spouse1 saw how large the account was becoming, spouse1 began to spend the money on all kinds of goods, *services, and causes which seemed necessary and worthwhile! However, spouse1 didn't want to be caught in a lie, so spouse1 began adding personal IOUs to the account to replace the money which was spent. These IOUs weren't backed by anything other than their future earnings. Eventually, spouse2 discovered that the retirement savings account had all been spent and confronted spouse1. How are we going to be able to retire?*

Over the years of deception, spouse1 had time to hatch an alternative plan for paying for their retirement. The plan required that their two children and their spouses put 6% of their income per year into the parent's retirement plan. This would provide $6,000 per year of the $38,000 needed by the parents. Unfortunately, $6,000 per year wasn't going to be enough. If only spouse1 had required that they have at least 13 children, the alternative plan would have worked. So spouse1 got more creative. Spouse1 realized that by the time they retired, the family should have four grandchildren and those grandchildren and their spouses would be over age 20 and working. If the grandchildren were each required to contribute $3,000 per year, another $12,000 per year could be added to their retirement. That would bring the total funds supplied by the children and grandchildren to $18,000 per year, which was still less than half of what was needed. Spouse1

*was still in a bind and needed another source of
funding. Finally, spouse1 remembered that the
family had good credit. They could borrow the additional $20,000 per year which was needed to
fund their retirement. The only downside was that
the children and grandchildren would have to co-
sign for the loan. The amount borrowed over the
20 years of retirement would be $400,000. After
20 years of borrowing at 5% interest, the children
and grandchildren would owe over $660,000.
Spouse1 realized that this was a heavy burden to
place on their children and grandchildren, but
hid that fact from them. Spouse1 didn't want
to lose the love of spouse2 or the children and
grandchildren.*

This is fundamentally the story of Social Security.
You may not want to call this a Ponzi scheme, but
it sure appears like one, because all the retirement
investment money was spent.

In this analogy, spouse1 is the federal government politicians who spent all of the retirement
money of the American families for multitudes of
government programs, services, payoffs, and other
really worthwhile causes, so they believe. We are
just now reaching the time when this story's parents are retiring and the real problem is present-
ing itself. Do we borrow in order to pay for the parent's retirement, which makes the problem worse

year after year? Do we double the amount which the children and grandchildren will be required to pay from 6% to 12%? Even at double, this will only provide a retirement for the parents and not build up any savings for the children and grandchildren. To build up savings for the next generations, the amount required for Social Security will need to be tripled to 18%, for a period of about 20 years, until an adequate surplus can be built. Possibly, the amounts paid to the parents can be reduced significantly through inflation. At the current real inflation rate, the amount paid to the parents can be cut in half in about 10 years or less. The answer is likely a combination of all of the above and even more ideas. This retirement deficit problem can be solved, but the American people have to be told the truth. It will never be solved if we allow spouse1 to keep lying to spouse2, children, and grandchildren.

Don't believe the misinformation provided by the federal government about the Social Security "trust fund." They are IOUs which are paid through the labor of our children and grandchildren. Even though Social Security is currently a Ponzi scheme, the scheme can be changed so it will work if properly funded and managed. Never again allow the federal government bureaucrats to steal this money and spend it on their pet programs. Lock the politicians out of the funds and make sure the funds are invested for building America and earning a reasonable rate of return. It will only take a decade or two of sacrifice and this problem can be resolved. However, we need politicians who are willing to tell us the truth and not continue to deceive us in order to save their own jobs. Spouse1 needs to become honest with the family and tell them that the parents' retirement funds were spent.

The steps needed to restore and save Social Security are as follows.

1) **Separate Social Security funding** completely from general tax revenues. Do not allow federal government politicians to spend these funds for anything other than retirement. The Social Security government agency should be given complete control over the payroll taxes collected, surplus funds to invest, and retirements paid. Congress should be restricted from gaining access to these payroll taxes or influencing how surplus funds are invested. Surplus funds should be invested in the U.S. and invested to maximize returns. Social Security administrative costs should be paid out of the investment returns. Congress should only have control over the pay scales and bonus payments made to employees within the Social Security administrative staff.

2) **Replenish the Social Security trust fund** over the next 20 years using federal revenue from the feder-

al wealth tax, wealth-increase tax, and 100% of the funds from the one-time wealth-increase tax. The trust fund value replenished should include all the payroll taxes collected and a yearly interest of 5% on those taxes, dating back 30 years. The Social Security agency should invest all excess Social Security funds, not immediately paid to retirees, into stocks and bonds of U.S. companies and U.S. federal, state, and local governments bonds for building America. The investments should earn a competitive rate of return.

3) **Change ownership of Social Security funds from the federal government to the individual contributors.** Calculate current values for Social Security contributors based upon the total amounts they paid into Social Security plus an investment return of 5% per year, minus funds that they have been paid by Social Security. This will become the initial Social Security balances for contributors.

Collect a percentage of employees' wages, as done now, for funding retirements. Currently, Social Security collects 6.2% of each employee's wages up to $106,800. The employee's company is required to match that 6.2%. The payroll taxes should be changed as follows.

1. Require an employee's company to increase each employee's wages by 6.2%, up to $106,800.

2. Remove the requirement for an employee's company to match the employee's payroll taxes by 6.2%, up to $106,800.

3. Collect 12.4% of an employee's wages, up to $106,800, and credit that total amount to the employee's account for retirement.

With the implementation of these changes, the payroll taxes paid to Social Security, the costs for a company, and the net pay received by each employee will not change. The primary benefit is that each employee will see the total amount which is being paid into their retirement and their retirement balance will be increased by this total amount. At the end of every year, Social Security should provide each person with a year-end net value of their retirement based upon their last year's ending balance, plus this year's total payroll taxes paid, plus this year's net investment earnings on the balance. Each person will know, on a yearly basis, the total value of their retirement and will be able to watch it grow. They will also know that the balance shown is their money and will not be taken and spent by the federal government on other programs.

4) **Allow self-employed individuals to voluntarily participate** in Social Security or let them save for their own retirements. The amount saved is determined by each individual, not dictated by

a nanny state. If the Social Security program is changed, such that the payroll taxes paid-in are really the retirement funds of the payer, and those funds will be professionally managed in order to obtain maximum conservative returns, many of the self-employed will want to participate. If they prefer to invest for their own retirements, they should be allowed that option.

5) **Future payouts are determined by each person's account balance** using the time-value-of-money. Professional investment managers will need to be hired by Social Security to manage the Social Security trust fund. They will be chartered to invest these funds into conservative investments, like bonds, which will maximize the returns and to invest in companies and government bonds which will help build America. The Social Security trust fund value will increase each year based on the investment returns obtained by these Social Security trust fund managers.

The Social Security program should be designed to allow each individual to start collecting as early as age 62, or later if desired, but not before age 62. The default payment amount should be based on a 20-year payout, using a 5% rate of return. Each individual can select a longer payout period, if desired, but the amount collected per month will be reduced in accordance with the increased payout years. A person will receive monthly payments from Social Security until all of their retirement value is consumed. At that time, their retirement payments will stop. If a person expects to live until age 100, the payout years should be selected which will provide an income until then. If an individual dies before age 62, the heirs will receive the retirement value of that individual. If the individual dies after age 62, but before collecting all their retirement value, the heirs will receive the remaining value.

If a spouse dies before age 62, the family will receive the Social Security retirement value of that spouse. If a spouse dies at a young age, this value may not be enough to meet the family's needs. Therefore, term life insurance policies may need to be included as a cost for each participant in Social Security, unless that individual has adequate life insurance coverage. The life insurance amount should be adequate to meet the family's need for a predetermined period of time. The amount of life insurance needed will likely decrease over time and eventually reach zero.

6) **Eliminate all payouts for Supplemental Social Security**. Social Security should be a **retirement program only.** The needs of the poor and/or disabled should be met using the taxes collected by the federal, state, and/or local governments, and

the welfare programs which these governments put into place. This should not be a function of Social Security.

The people currently collecting SSI will need to be transitioned into other government funded programs which should be set-up to meet their needs. It appears that federal government politicians saw the large surpluses paid into Social Security each year and decided that this was the perfect way to pay for their very expensive welfare programs. Unfortunately, those large surpluses no longer exist.

7) **Move all government employee pensions into Social Security and eliminate their separate pensions**. U.S. companies have been eliminating their private pension plans at a fast pace in recent years due to the huge liabilities incurred. Most U.S. companies have replaced their retirement pensions with small percentage matching payments into 401K retirement plans. Within private industry today, most employees will not receive a pension from their company. Their only retirement will be based upon Social Security and what they contributed to their 401K plan, with a small percentage retirement match by their company, and the investment returns they are able to achieve on the 401K savings.

Government employees have been paying into Social Security since 1984. Prior to 1984, they did not pay into Social Security, but paid into their own pension plan called the Civil Service Retirement System (CSRS). After 1984, the Federal Employees Retirement System (FERS) was created to coordinate their pensions with Social Security. Federal employees then paid into Social Security and FERS. As a third retirement benefit, federal employees can put $16,500 per year into a Thrift Savings Plan, similar to a 401K. The pension program for government employees is superior to the pension plans, if any, of most workers in the private sector. Also, government employee pensions are the only pensions which increase with the cost of living. This is unfair to those working in the private sector, since they are paying for the government pensions.

There have been many news stories lately of pension abuse occurring at the state and local government levels. When public sector workers are given keys to the treasury, through their votes and support of particular politicians, there is a human-nature tendency to grab all the money they can. Laws and rules are implemented which provide huge benefits to these public workers. As a recent example in Illinois, ten administrators retired, started drawing pension checks and returned immediately as contract employees, a process known as double-dipping. A school administrator in Illinois makes a combined $409,000 a year in pension payments and salary for overseeing a public boarding school. In California, New York, Texas, Florida, and Michigan, at least 66,000 government retirees also receive taxpayer-funded paychecks. Some teacher's union leaders in Illinois earn a guaranteed pension of $100,000 per year based on a contribution of $25,000 per year for four years from them and their employers. A former president of the NEA earns a retirement of $20,000 per month. State governments currently have a combined $690 billion in unfunded pension liabilities.

Federal politicians have created generous pension plans for themselves. Congressmen and Senators can retire at age 50 with 20 years of service, age 62 with 5 years of service, and at any age with 25 years of service.

It is time to totally eliminate the pension plans which politicians have provided for themselves and to move the pensions of government employees completely into Social Security. Social Security should be the pension program for all American workers, not just for those who *don't* have special access to government power. In order to compensate government employees for their CSRS or FERS pension values earned to date, the pension value for each employee should be calculated, transferred to the Social Security program, and added to their Social Security balance. The new balance will be their money. A limit should be placed on the pension monetary value to offset extremely large pensions that were provided to some highly compensated government employees.

Now is the time to restructure Social Security, put it on a solid financial footing, and make it the retirement system envy of the world. It can be accomplished with some common sense changes. Our children and grandchildren will thank us for saving Social Security for them and providing a secure retirement system for all Americans.

CHAPTER 3:

TERM LIMITS ON POLITICAL OFFICES

Impose term limits on politicians at all levels of government, and at the federal level through a Constitutional Amendment.

Today, in America, there is a ruling class of elite politicians at the federal level. They are career politicians who are power brokers for decades. They provide themselves with very expensive perks at taxpayer expense, including lucrative retirement plans, exempt themselves from the laws they pass, and literally rule the nation from Washington D.C. They seem primarily concerned with collecting campaign funds from the nation's wealthy, obfuscating issues, protecting campaign donors, and worrying more about their next election than what is best for the country. They are not the citizens' government as was originally conceived by our Founding Fathers.

It is time for the American people to take back control of the country from this ruling class. It is time to return to a citizens' government. America, as we have known it, is changing rapidly in many disturbing ways. What kind of America do you want to leave for your children and grandchildren? It is time to make changes and some of these changes are as follows.

1) **Limit members of the Congress, Senate, and Presidency to one term in office**. Per the U.S. Constitution, Congressmen are elected to a two-year term, Senators to a six-year term, and Presidents to a four-year term. In 1951, the 22nd Amendment to the Constitution was passed which restricted the President of the United States to a maximum of two terms. This was done after the presidency of Franklin D. Roosevelt. FDR was the first President in American history to serve more than two terms. The American people became concerned about a President serving too long and becoming too powerful.

The 22nd Amendment was on the right track and a step in the right direction. It is time for the American people to demand another Constitutional Amendment which will limit U.S. Congressmen, Senators, and Presidents to one term, and only once in their lifetime for each office. Significant benefits will be obtained by making this change. Wealthy campaign donors, who have powerful influences over long-term politicians, will be less influential on those only serving one term. This is because the one-term politicians will not be running for re-election and, therefore, won't need to sell their votes for large campaign contributions. The one-term politicians will focus more on the nation's needs and less on their re-election campaigns. Special retirement programs and the associated costs can be eliminated for one-term politicians, since their service to the nation will be short and they can return to their normal professions or jobs. One-term politicians will be held accountable by their communities for the laws passed and rejected during their short time in office. They will not have time to lose touch with their constituents. They will not become a permanent resident of Washington D.C. and will not be enticed into the ruling class thinking that all power should emanate from Washington D.C. Once elected, the one-term politicians will sense an urgency to accomplish their goals, which will likely be a benefit to the nation rather than to their re-election. The nation needs to be run by a citizens' government, not controlled by a ruling elite class.

2) **Limit Supreme Court justices to 12 years in office (three presidential terms)**. The nine Supreme

Court justices of the U.S. are the epitome of a small elite ruling class. Their influence on the nation's laws is enormous. At times, when the court is split 5-to-4, one justice has the power to make a ruling which will have major impacts on the entire country, which the country must obey, even if the majority of people in the country disagree, and even if the legislative and executive branches of government disagree. To make matters worse, there is no accountability. A Supreme Court justice is not bound by the Constitution, since the Supreme Court justices interpret the Constitution's meaning. In recent history, activist justices have effectively made laws from the bench, ignoring their Constitutional limits. Even if the legislative and executive branches were to override their judicial law by passing a legitimate law, the justices can override that law as unconstitutional based on the whim of one justice.

A Supreme Court justice can have more power and influence within the U.S. than any other federal government official, including the President. This is because a Supreme Court justice is appointed for life. A single justice, assuming a split court, can rule the country for a generation. The power of a single Supreme Court justice needs to be reduced. The following are recommendations for limiting a Supreme Court justice's power.

The U.S. Constitution does not specify the total number of Supreme Court justices. The quantity can be increased or decreased by the President. A Constitutional Amendment is needed to set the quantity of justices. Since the number of Supreme Court justices has been nine for many decades, the quantity should be set at nine. Within this Constitutional Amendment, additional changes and restrictions should be included.

1. Term limits need to be imposed for each Supreme Court justice. The term limit should be set to twelve years and allow a justice to serve only one term.

2. The President currently chooses a Supreme Court justice candidate only when a sitting justice dies or resigns, because there is no term limit. The Senate then confirms or rejects the new candidate. A new justice is seated once chosen by the President and confirmed by the Senate. With the new proposed term limits of twelve years, each President will select three new Supreme Court justice candidates and the Senate will confirm or reject these candidates. The selection and confirmation process should occur during the fourth year of a presidential term. Once confirmed, the three new justices will replace the three term-ending justices at the start of the next President's

term. If a Supreme Court justice, who is not at the end of a twelve-year term, resigns or dies, a new justice candidate will need to be selected by the previous President who selected that justice. The new justice candidate will need to be confirmed by the current Senate. This new replacement justice will serve out the term of the replaced justice. The replacement justice will not be allowed as a candidate for a new 12-year term. If the previous President is unable to select a justice candidate, then the previous Vice President will select a justice candidate. If neither the President nor the Vice President is able to select a justice candidate, the position will remain open until the year for which it is to be filled by a new President.

3. The current Supreme Court justices, who were appointed to life terms, will have their terms reduced to comply with the new Amendment. The three justices who have served the longest time will be the first three justices replaced. The next three justices who have served the next longest time will be the second three justices replaced. And finally the last three justices, who have served the shortest time, will be replaced. This should be completed over a period of twelve years.

4. Activist Supreme Court justices are, in effect, making laws from the bench. They are not bound by the Constitution, but by their interpretation of the Constitution. The Constitutional Amendment, which applies term limits to judges, should also include changes to rein-in this activity. Supreme Court justices should be restricted from making decisions which become laws unto themselves. If the Supreme Court believes that a law is needed, they should require Congress to pass or reject that law and the President to approve or veto it. As an example, the Supreme Court should not have the ability to rule that gay marriage is legal within the U.S. If the U.S. wants to legalize gay marriage, a law should be passed by Congress and approved by the President. The Supreme Court should have the power to force the legislative and executive branches to resolve the issue, but not to resolve it themselves. A new law of the land should not be enacted just because of a Supreme Court ruling.

The example given is not a good example, since the legalization of gay marriages should not be an issue for the federal government. The federal government does not have authority over the definition of marriage, based on the Constitution. This is an issue which should be addressed on a state by state basis, which is currently happening across the country.

3) **Limit state and local governments' elected offices to one term**. If the massive control and power of the federal government are reduced and power is transferred to the state governments, then the state governments may suffer from the same lobbying influences which are plaguing the federal government. Setting term limits on politicians at the state level will become more important. It will be up to the citizens of each state to implement term limit changes on their governors and legislators. This will need to be accomplished on a state by state basis.

4) **Require five years** between when a politician leaves office to the time they can benefit, as an employee or consultant, from a company which specifically benefited from legislation passed during the politician's term in office. The purpose of this requirement is to reduce cronyism votes and conflicts of interest. Also, do not allow gifts or other compensation to be provided to the politician from that company, subsidiary, officer, or any other closely linked entity. Very strict rules are currently placed on government employees regarding pay-

ments and gifts received. These same rules need to be applied to politicians with the additional five year requirement.

It is critical that stringent term limits be enacted for our future elected politicians. Many of today's problems within the U.S. can be linked to career politicians and their abuse of power. The federal politicians' drive to centralize government power and move all control to Washington D.C. is a direct result of not having term limits. This allows an elite group of federal politicians to rule the nation from Washington D.C. for decades and possibly for a generation. It encourages them to lust after more power and control. It encourages them to spend vast sums of money the nation doesn't have for buying votes in their districts or states. It encourages them to succumb to the influences of large campaign donors to ensure their re-election. The results of their abuse of power and the influence of large campaign donors are obvious today. It is time to limit the terms of all elected politicians. It is time to get back to a citizen's government.

CHAPTER 4:

MEDICARE AND MEDICAID

The federal government's liability for Medicare and Medicaid is growing at a rate which will eventually bankrupt the nation. These programs, as they currently stand, are not sustainable for the long term. It is important to provide quality health care to all U.S. citizens, but it must be accomplished in a way which is reasonable and affordable. The best way to describe the problem is with an analogy, called the *economics of free bread.*

Assume that the federal government decided to make bread available to all its citizens at no cost. On the surface this appears to be a very humanitarian policy. Everyone will have access to the free bread and, therefore, no one will starve. The government will pay for the bread through taxes and deficit spending. What are the consequences of this new free bread policy?

As an example, let's say that the average family normally purchased two loaves of bread each week. They were careful in using the bread and even consumed the heels in order to maximum the benefits of their purchases. Hence, there was no waste of bread. The only waste was the bread wrapper. The total consumption of bread in the U.S. was well known and farmers set aside a small portion of their farm land for growing wheat, rye, oats, and other grains to meet the bread demand. The price for these grains was limited by consumer demand of other food products, like corn chips, potato chips, vegetables, etc. Each of these different food products had to compete. If the price of bread went too high in comparison to other foods, the family would purchase less bread and reduce the demand.

Once bread became free, the average family realized that they didn't need to limit themselves to two loaves of bread per week and began to take ten loaves per week from the grocery store. They no longer needed to eat the heels and, in fact, even decided that they didn't want to eat day-old bread. They wanted nothing but the best bread and the freshest. If all the bread in a loaf wasn't consumed in a given day, the bread was thrown out and added to the trash. The family also decided that they could spend less of their hard-earned money for other food products, thus reducing the demand of those products.

The demand for free bread increased by five times and the demand for corn, potatoes, and other crops diminished. Thus, farmers changed the crops they planted to meet the new demands. Grain production went up five times while other crops were reduced in proportion. The price of grain increased dramatically during this period of time, costing the federal government ten times what they had originally estimated.

As time passed, families decided that bread could be used in many other ways, since it was free. They started feeding it to the wildlife in their neighborhoods. Farmers began using it as feed for their livestock. Gardeners and grain farmers began to use it as fertilizer. People found numerous new uses for bread and the demand skyrocketed.

The demand for free bread increased beyond the farmers' capacity to grow enough grain to meet the demand. All farm land was shifted to growing grain for free bread and the demand increased beyond production capacity. The government's cost skyrocketed even more. The government's cost for free bread program jumped to 100 times its original estimates and continued to rise. The government couldn't keep up with the increasing costs, even with massive tax increases and massive *deficit spending. The economics of free bread eventually bankrupted the federal government and the country collapsed.*

This is really the story of free health care in America. In America's past, the family sought medical care when they felt it was absolutely necessary. The health care obtained was limited by what they could afford. The medical providers kept their fees low to accommodate the ability of their patients to pay.

Over time, however, the concept of "pay for services" was diluted by the prevalence of medical insurance. For a small monthly insurance fee the American family could obtain free health care. The fees of the medical providers were paid by the insurance company rather than by the family. This opened the door to the concept of free medical care. Families began to request much more medical care than they had in the past. Because of this increased demand and the limited supply of medical providers, the medical providers started charging much higher rates for their services. This caused the cost of the insurance to increase dramatically. The higher the monthly insurance costs, the more medical care was requested. Since the cost of the medical care provided was disconnected from the cost to the patient, patients demanded the absolute best medical care available and the amount of care requested was unlimited. This, in turn, caused even more of a medical provider shortage and the costs continued to climb. As a result, the monthly medical insurance costs soared. It will reach the point where only a few can afford medical insurance or medical care. In 2011, the annual premiums for employer-sponsored health insurance surged 9% and surpassed $15,000 per family. Since the average family makes $50,000 per year, health insurance premiums have reached 30% of the average family's income. This is more than the $10,000 Joe Average paid for income taxes, Social Security, and Medicare combined, as shown in a previous chapter. The health care insurance costs have more than doubled since 2001.

Medicare and Medicaid were introduced to help deal with the increasing costs. The elderly, who were living on small incomes and needed the most care, could not afford the ever rising medical costs. They also couldn't afford the medical insurance. Likewise, the non-elderly poor could not afford the medical costs or insurance. Thus, the federal government stepped in to provide free, or almost free, medical care for these groups. It was the humanitarian thing to do. Unfortunately, adding these large groups into the free medical care system began to overwhelm the medical care providers. A larger and larger percentage of the U.S. work force was required to work in the medical field to meet the ever growing demand. More and more people could no longer afford the medical insurance and were added to the rolls of Medicaid and Medicare. The costs for these programs began to skyrocket. As in the case of the *economics of free bread*, the costs for these programs will eventually bankrupt the country.

Based on the belief that health insurance, Medicare, and Medicaid are not sustainable as is, what steps can be taken to rein-in the growth and costs of these programs and still provide the medical care needed? The following are suggested changes.

1) **Require at least a 20% payment for the total medical care from each patient**. In order to break the concept of "free bread", every consumer must be required to pay for a portion of all the health care which they receive. Families will then operate as normal consumers of medical care. They will only seek medical care when absolutely needed. They will seek the least cost care and, with the help of their doctors, they will decide what care is absolutely needed versus requesting the best and most expensive care known to mankind. This will decrease the total demand for medical care and likely make the care more affordable due to the decreased demand and increased competition.

What if a patient cannot afford 20% of the total cost for the medical care needed? A maximum limit can be set to 20% of a patient's income or 20% of a patient's wealth, whichever is higher. Beyond that amount, the insurance company, if a patient has medical insurance, or the government will need to cover the costs. All families have income or wealth in order to survive. Income from all sources, including wages, dividends, interest payments, trust fund payments, welfare payments, food stamps, housing allowances, etc., need to be included. For the self-employed, if their income is not known, base the limit on the value of their wealth.

The 20% payment for medical care and the 20% maximum limit on income or wealth can be called the 20/20 rule.

2) **Limit a doctor's liability for malpractice lawsuits**. The vast majorities of medical professionals are competent at their jobs and provide excellent care for their patients. As in any profession sometimes mistakes are made. The medical costs for all are increased significantly if a doctor can be sued for any and every mistake. The percentage of doctors who will be sued during their careers is estimated to be over 80%. Hence, doctors purchase very expensive malpractice insurance which is added to their medical costs. A method is needed to eliminate, or greatly reduce, malpractice lawsuits since lawyers'

fees add significantly to the cost of medical care. An alternative is to set-up a medical malpractice oversight agency. This agency will establish rules for awarding payments to patients who have been harmed and managing a malpractice fund for paying these awards. The malpractice fund will collect the malpractice insurance amounts currently paid by doctors. It is expected that the funds collected will be more than the payments awarded since lawyers' fees are removed. Also, the doctors' costs for defending themselves in a court-of-law are also removed. The fees collected each year from doctors will likely be reduced significantly over time. If any malpractice lawsuits are filed, they will be defended by the medical malpractice oversight agency.

In addition to creating a medical malpractice oversight agency, states could follow the example of Texas. In 2003, the Texas legislator passed a bill to limit the medical liability lawsuit maximum payments. Texas voters approved this bill under proposition 12 in order to ensure its legality. The medical insurance costs have been reduced dramatically since that passage.

3) **Have medical insurance companies establish a variety of medical insurance policies** which specifically define what medical care is covered and what is not. Medical care which is considered very expensive compared to the potential benefits

should be included in premium policies and the monthly rates priced accordingly. Medical care which is considered the minimum care required should be included in basic policies and priced much lower. With a range of well-defined options, patients can purchase the plan they can afford and which best meets their needs. These plans need to be made available nationwide rather than limited to specific states. This will provide the most competition. Medicare and Medicaid should offer these basic plans to their members. They should allow their members to choose any upgraded plan that they want to purchase. Once a plan level is chosen (premium down to basic), at least three years notice must be given to move up or down in the coverage level. This will help deter people from purchasing a basic plan when healthy and then upgrading immediately to a premium plan when they are sick.

4) **Reduce medical paperwork required** by insurance companies, Medicare, and Medicaid. An ever growing medical expense is the paperwork required for doctors and hospitals to get paid. Hospitals have to account for every service provided, device used, and item consumed. Since hospitals are paid by the service, device, or item, the more tests run and the more pills prescribed, the more the hospital is paid. This adds significantly

to medical costs by requiring all this to be tracked and charged. If any mistakes are made on the paperwork, the hospital or doctor doesn't get paid until the paperwork is corrected. This provides incentives for insurance companies to make their forms complex and change the rules periodically, thus delaying payments. New and simpler methods are needed which allow hospitals and doctors to charge at a top-down level for the medical care provided. Insurance companies, Medicare, and Medicaid should establish standard rates paid for specific illness care and eliminate the need for specific details of the care.

The changes described in the first four categories above will significantly reduce the demand for medical services, create an environment of competition, and reduce overhead costs. This will help bring medical costs down and make medical care more affordable for everyone. It will reduce the *economics of free bread.*

5) **Funding and expenses for Medicare and Medicaid (M&M)** need to be separated from the general federal tax revenues and expenses, just like proposed for Social Security. The revenue and expenses need to be managed independently by a health care "trust fund" management agency. There are several sources of funding which can be used for the M&M trust fund. First, families who

participate in the government plans should pay a monthly fee to participate, similar to buying insurance. Second, all cigarette and tobacco taxes should go into the M&M trust fund. Third, the U.S. should seriously consider legalizing drugs, like marijuana, regulate the manufacturing of these drugs, and collect taxes on them. 100% of these taxes should go into the M&M trust fund. Fourth, an M&M sales tax should be added to processed foods and drinks which are proven to be unhealthy. For example, foods and drinks high in sugar, like desserts and colas, and high in salt, like potato chips and canned vegetables. Fifth, an M&M sales tax should be added to alcoholic beverages. All of these taxes should be collected for the M&M trust fund only.

The sales tax percentages on the various foods and drinks considered unhealthy should be set to a percentage which will cover the forecasted health care costs for the coming year. Tax rates can be adjusted up or down each year to meet the actual health care costs.

CHAPTER 5:

ELIMINATE FEDERAL GOVERNMENT DEBT

The total federal debt at the end of fiscal year 2010 was $13.4 trillion. So, how much is $13.4 trillion? Do your eyes glaze over when politicians talk about spending billions and trillions of dollars? Is it difficult to grasp the size of $1 billion, $100 billion, or $1 trillion? Let's adjust the amounts into terms which U.S. citizens understand very well, monthly payments and hourly wages. The following table provides a simple conversion chart. For each $100 billion spent by the federal government, the cost to each U.S. citizen is $320 and to the average family is $1,216, assuming 3.8 persons per average family. This equates to a family expense of $101 per month or $0.58 per hour of family wages. In 2010, the federal government spent $3.7 trillion, or $11,857 per U.S. citizen, or $45,057 per family. That equates to an expense of $3,755 per month or consumption of

$21.66 per hour of family wages. An approximate rule of thumb which can be used is that for each $1 billion spent by the federal government per year, it will cost the average U.S. family $1 per month.

U.S. Federal Spending	Spent (in billions)	Average per person	Average per family	Family Monthly	Family Hourly
Each $100 billion	$100	$320	$1,216	$101	$0.58
Each $1 trillion	$1,000	$3,205	$12,179	$1,015	$5.86
Spent in 2010	$3,700	$11,857	$45,057	$3,755	$21.66

The average family income for 2010 is shown in the following table. As you can see, the average family income is $4,167 per month or $24.04 per hour of wages. The federal government needs 90% of all the family wages to cover its current spending. Since it cannot tax wages that much, it has become very creative in its ways to collect money. It has created numerous methods for taxing, but still fall short. Hence, that is why it makes up the difference by running a deficit, printing money, and decreasing the value of the U.S. dollar. Have you seen the changes in the price of gold, food, and gasoline?

2010 U.S. Federal	Income (in billions)	Average per person	Average per family	Family Monthly	Family Hourly
Average Income	$4,100	$13,158	$50,000	$4,167	$24.04

You have probably heard the news media talk about entitlement costs. The following table shows that about $2.5 trillion was spent on entitlements in 2010. The costs are increasing rapidly and will double in the next ten years. Interest on the debt will increase about four times the current level in the next ten years. Based on the current estimates, the total cost in 2020 will be over $5 trillion.

2010 Federal Spending for Entitlements and Interest	Spent (in billions)	Average per person	Average per family	Family Monthly	Family Hourly
Social Security and Supplemental	$721	$2,312	$8,786	$732	$4.22
Medicare	$457	$1,465	$5,567	$464	$2.68
Medicaid	$284	$912	$3,466	$289	$1.67
Income security	$363	$1,163	$4,419	$368	$2.12
Unemployment benefits	$194	$623	$2,367	$197	$1.14
Veterans benefits	$125	$399	$1,516	$126	$0.73
Federal employees retirement	$121	$387	$1,471	$123	$0.71
Interest on debt	$188	$602	$2,288	$191	$1.10
Total entitlements and interest	$2,453	$7,863	$29,880	$2,490	$14.37

As shown in the following table, today, in America, there are currently about 115 million people working in private and government sector jobs. There are about 80 million people collecting checks from the federal government for Social Security (retirement), Supplemental Social Security (welfare), and unemployment benefits. That equates to seven people collecting checks for every ten people working. Taxes will need to increase significantly to support these entitlements. Thomas Jefferson said, "The democracy will cease to exist when you take away from those who are willing to work and give to those who would not."

U. S. Population Breakdown	Number (millions)	Percent
Total Citizens	312	100%
Taxpayers	112	35.9%
Retired and SSI Recipients	66	21.1%
Food Stamp Recipients	47	15.1%
U. S. Workforce	**139**	**44.6%**
Officially Unemployed	14	9.9%
Actually Unemployed	25	17.7%
Federal Employees	4	3.1%
State and Local Employees	16	11.4%
Private Sector Employees	95	67.9%

In addition to entitlement spending and interest on the debt, the Federal government also spends money on its current programs, which is called discretionary spending. The discretionary spending for 2010 is shown in the following table. The discretionary spending was about half the 2010 entitlement spending.

Discretionary Federal Spending	Spent (in billions)	Average per person	Average per family	Family Monthly	Family Hourly
Military	$719	$2,305	$8,759	$730	$4.21
Department of Education	$108	$347	$1,319	$110	$0.63
Highways	$73	$233	$885	$74	$0.43
Health Research and Regulation	$65	$209	$794	$66	$0.38
Justice Administration	$55	$176	$669	$56	$0.32
International Affairs	$51	$164	$623	$52	$0.30
Nat. Resource & Environment	$47	$151	$574	$48	$0.28
Training, Employ., Soc Svcs	$34	$110	$418	$35	$0.20
General Science and Tech.	$33	$106	$403	$34	$0.19
General Government	$29	$94	$357	$30	$0.17
Community and Regional Dev.	$29	$92	$350	$29	$0.17
Farm Subsidies	$27	$85	$323	$27	$0.16
Federal Employment Health	$23	$73	$277	$23	$0.13
Air Transport	$23	$73	$277	$23	$0.13
Energy	$19	$61	$232	$19	$0.11
Other	$39	$125	$475	$40	$0.23
Credits for Dep. Ins. & Receipts	-$106	-$341	-$1,296	-$108	-$0.62
Total	$1,267	$4,063	$15,439	$1,287	$7.42

The federal government collected $2.2 trillion in 2010, but spent $3.7 trillion. It borrowed $1.5 trillion of the money spent. The $2.2 trillion of revenue did not even cover the 2010 entitlement and interest costs of $2.5 trillion. Hence, the federal government borrowed more than its entire discretionary spending in 2010. If the federal government was shut down the U.S. would still be running a deficit. Unfortunately, entitlement spending will continue to increase significantly as previously stated. If entitlements reach $5 trillion by 2020 and the discretionary budget remains at the 2010 level of $1.3 trillion, the federal government will need to collect $6.3 trillion in taxes, or about three times the amount collected in 2010.

The federal government's deficit spending has been going on for a long time. However, the deficit amounts are rapidly increasing. The current debt is shown in the following table.

Federal Debt	Federal debt (in billions)	Average debt per person	Average debt per family
Total debt at end of 2010	$13,400	$43,000	$163,000
Increase in debt in 2011	$1,400	$4,000	$15,000
Total debt at end of 2011	$14,800	$47,000	$178,000

The current government forecasts show an average deficit of about $1 trillion per year through 2020. That will be added to the current deficit and shown in the following table. The debt will be almost double for our children in the next nine years. Each family will owe over one-quarter of a million dollars just for the federal debt.

Federal Debt in 2020	Federal debt (in billions)	Average debt per person	Average debt per family
Debt inherited by your children	$24,000	$77,000	$293,000

The estimated liabilities for entitlement programs are shown in the following table. This does not include the additional liability which will be incurred with Obama health care. The average family's liability will be greater than $1 million.

Estimated Liability for Social Security / Medicare	Liability (in billions)	Average per person	Average per family	Family Monthly	Family Hourly
Funding gaps in Medicare	$100,000	$320,459	$1,217,744	$2,537	$14.64
Funding gaps in Soc. Sec.	$15,000	$48,069	$182,662	$381	$2.20
Total	$115,000	$368,528	$1,400,406	$2,918	$16.84

The purpose of this information is to help clear some of the fog when politicians talk about spending billions and trillions of dollars. Each trillion spent is equivalent to the average American family spending about $1,000 per month, or being taxed $1,000 per month, to pay for the government spending.

Some ideas for controlling entitlement costs were presented in previous sections. This section will address methods to stop the growing federal debt and change it to a surplus over time.

1) **Balance the federal budget**. Federal politicians seem unable to control their urges for spending money on programs which they feel are vital, important, maybe important, not very important, a waste, and obsolete. Politicians are also heavily influenced by lobbyists who want money spent on their favorite programs, which usually benefit the lobbyists. Therefore, U.S. citizens need to help federal politicians control their urges to spend by demanding that a Constitutional Amendment be passed which requires balancing the budget each

year with the only exception being a *major world war*. The federal government needs to operate with a balanced budget requirement just like the states are required to do.

A balanced budget amendment will stop the nation's debt explosion, but will not pay-off the existing federal debt. Until the federal debt is eliminated, interest will need to be paid each year until the debt is zero. The interest payments could be put to better humanitarian use providing additional benefits to those who most need it, rather than payments to those who don't.

2) **Pay off the debt**. Within a new Constitutional Amendment which requires balancing the federal budget each year, there should also be a requirement to reduce the existing federal debt by 10% per year minimum and be completely paid-off within 10 years. The principle payment amount per year will be approximately $1.5 trillion. Congress should decide how this can best be done. It may be through a combination of methods. Increase the federal wealth or wealth-increase tax percentages, reduce entitlement and discretionary spending, and sell government assets and services. Once the debt is eliminated, Congress should accumulate a surplus of funds up to one year's budget. The surplus funds should be invested in U.S. businesses, state or local governments' projects, and earn

interest. The interest collected can help pay for future federal government expenses.

If the federal government is required to balance its budget and pay off its debt, the U.S. dollar will become the most stable currency in the world. The U.S. dollar will remain the world's primary currency and the world won't need to switch to a new world currency or gold. The inflation rate caused by the U.S. government will be dramatically reduced, and possibly to zero.

CHAPTER 6:

REDUCE MILITARY SPENDING

In 2010, military spending was the largest discretionary federal spending expense at $719 billion. This equates to an average monthly cost per U.S. family of $679. The primary responsibility of the federal government is to protect American citizens from external threats. The U.S. military is the strongest and most powerful military force in the world and the American people benefit from its protection. America has not been attacked by another foreign military power since the Japanese bombed Pearl Harbor. The U.S. military has done a superb job of protecting American citizens and their interests. However, as with any large federal government spending program, savings can be found which will not have a significant impact on the protection provided by the U.S. military.

Throughout history, countries with the strongest military power have created global empires using their military power. The Romans grew their empire from 300 B.C. until about 500 A.D. Later, the British grew their empire from about 1600 until World War II. Since the end of World War II, America has had the strongest military power in the world and, as such, has established military bases throughout the world. In 117 A.D., Rome had 37 major bases to police its empire. In 1898, the British had 36 major naval bases to police its empire. In 2005, America had 38 large and medium size bases, with 737 military bases worldwide. In 2010, America's military bases were in 135 countries and America accounted for about 40% of the world's total military spending, much larger than any other country. Has America become the latest global empire and needs these bases to police the world? America can no longer afford to be the policeman of the world. It is time to shut down many of the worldwide military bases and reduce the federal spending accordingly.

In 2005, the American foreign military bases were estimated to have a minimal value of $127 billion. The total personnel who comprised the military, including civil service and local support, were about 2.5 million people and approximately 0.5 million, or 20%, were stationed at foreign bases. The estimated cost in 2010 for the military personnel was approximately $154 billion per year of which $30 billion (20%) per year is for personnel assigned to foreign bases. The cost of operations and maintenance was $283 billion of which 20% is $56 billion.

If many of these foreign bases were closed, the increased danger to the American people would be minimal. Assuming that at least 50% of the bases could be closed with little, if any, increased danger, the potential savings would be $40 billion per year. With a thorough financial analysis, the potential savings will likely be more. It is time for the federal government to review costs of the American empire and find the best ways to reduce them without adding danger to the American people. America can no longer afford its empire.

CHAPTER 7:

ELIMINATE THE DEPARTMENT OF EDUCATION

In 2010, the second largest discretionary federal expenditure was $108 billion for the Department of Education (ED). The Department of Education Organization Act was signed into law by President Jimmy Carter in 1979 and the ED began operating in 1980. This act was considered by many to be unconstitutional since the education of American children is not identified in the U.S. Constitution as a responsibility of the federal government. Throughout America's history, the education of children was managed at the state and local government levels. However, those Americans who want a very powerful central federal government are in favor of the federal government's intrusion into all areas of American life, regardless of the limitations imposed by the Constitution. The Commerce Clause of the Constitution is generally interpreted by this elitist group of Americans to justify the federal government's intrusions into and control of any and all aspects of American life. It is easier for them to impose their will at the federal level than having to control American lives at the state level, since it will require at least 50 times the effort. America's Founding Fathers were concerned about the centralization of power because they had seen the abuses which it causes. That is why they divided power between multiple branches of the federal government and limited the power of the federal government, stating that all powers not specifically given to the federal government are given to the states. Individual liberties and freedom are put at risk when power is concentrated into the hands of a few. History has shown this over and over.

The U.S. does not need and can no longer afford the Department of Education. The federal budget can be reduced by over $100 billion per year, or $100 per month savings for the average American family. This savings will be a small step in helping to balance the federal government's budget.

Prior to the creation of the Department of Education, America had the best education system in the world. Today, America is rated below many third world countries. It cannot be directly shown that America's poor education rating was caused by the ED, but it is obvious that there has been little benefit from the ED.

The ED primarily imposes its will on state governments by offering funds, but with strings attached. By 2011, discretionary funds for the ED were increased to $70 billion. Federal taxes are collected from the taxpayers of each state and then some of that money is given back to the state, if the state will comply with requirements imposed by the ED. Many times, the costs to comply are more expensive than the funds provided. Many times, the funds do not benefit the children, but benefit the teachers' unions. Because of ED, politics and political favors are now a major part of America's education system. The funds spent for political favors will be better utilized on resources which educate our children.

The establishment of the Department of Education in 1980 should be viewed as a trial program to improve the education of children in America. Over the last 30 years, this trial program has failed miserably. The world ranking of America's education system has dramatically decreased. It is time for the trial program to end.

Once a program is started by the federal government, it has difficulty shutting that program down, even when the major benefits of the program have been accomplished, the program has failed, or the program becomes obsolete. The federal government needs to become as good at shutting down programs as it is at starting them. We can no longer afford paying for completed, failed, and obsolete programs. America's limited tax revenue can be better spent in other areas.

When the responsibility for educating our children is given back to the states, each of the 50 states will be able to experiment with ideas for improving the education system. The best ideas from each state for enhancing our children's education can then be adopted by the other states. This will create a nationwide environment where 50 different ideas can be tried simultaneously, and the successful methods identified and implemented much faster than relying on the federal government to get it right. The federal government had problems with managing the "cash for clunkers" program. What is the likelihood that they will be successful in making our education system the best in the world again?

CHAPTER 8

INCENTIVIZE SAVING MONEY IN GOVERNMENT PROGRAMS

A federal government program spending rule, followed for decades, has been that if all budgeted funds are not spent on a program, the program's budget for the following year will be reduced. The incentive for federal government program managers is to spend every penny in order to maximize next year's budget. This rule leads to maximum spending and penalizes those who don't. Thus, the goal of every government program is to spend 100% of the budget allocated and be awarded a larger budget the next year. This rule leads to ever increasing federal government spending with very few, if any, reductions. This rule would bankrupt companies in the private sector and is bankrupting

America. New federal government spending rules are needed to incentivize spending **less** rather than more. The following new rules are suggested as a replacement for the *maximum spending rule.*

Rule 1: Do not increase federal government program budgets from year to year. The primary reason budgets are increased each year is due to inflation. With the implementation of the tax policy changes and balanced budget amendment previously discussed in this book, federal government caused inflation will be eliminated. This will also eliminate the need for budgets to increase each year. Government employee salaries, benefits, and operating costs will be stabilized and likely established at long-term set levels. The need to plan for *inflation-caused* unknown, hard-to-predict, bogeyman cost increases will be eliminated.

Rule 2: Set a goal for each federal government program manager to reduce the cost of their program by 5% per year. Establish pay guidelines for all employees within a program based on this goal. A bonus of 1/2% of yearly pay will be paid to each employee for each 1% that spending is reduced, up to the 5% goal. If the 5% reduction goal is met, the employees will receive a 2.5% pay bonus. The immediate savings for the federal government is the other 2.5% of the 5% savings. The next year's budget for that program will be set to the reduced budget achieved. Thus, if the 5% goal was met, the budget for the following year would be reduced by the 5% savings. If only 2% was saved, then the budget would be reduced by 2%. This provides an incentive to reduce the federal government's budget each year. Each year's federal government cost savings would be accumulated year after year. The savings each year would be conserved for many future years.

Rule 3: Evaluate the benefits and effectiveness of each federal government program every year. Congress should establish a small evaluation group within each program to analyze, evaluate, report, and recommend changes for reducing costs and increasing benefits. The benefits recommendations should be based upon benefits for the general U.S. population and not for the benefits of specific groups within that population. For example, the federal government pays land owners for not growing crops on their land. Some very wealthy land owners, who own thousands of acres of land, are paid millions of dollars by the federal government for not growing crops on their land. It is likely that this program, which costs millions, benefits the general population very little, but benefits the wealthy land owners significantly. The evaluation group within this program will analyze the program, evaluate the benefits to the general population, report the results to Congress, and recommend proposed changes. Congress should be required to separately vote to accept or reject each program's individual recommendations. Compensation pay bonuses for the evaluation group should be based upon meeting pre-defined savings goals as determined by Congress. All of the savings proposals should then be consolidated into one bill which will be either signed or vetoed by the President.

CHAPTER 9:

MOVE POWER BACK TO THE STATES

Our Founding Fathers were concerned about too much power being given to the federal government. They knew from history that individual freedoms and liberties were lost when too much power is concentrated in the hands of one person or a small ruling class. They saw first hand how their individual rights were trampled by the King and ruling elites of England. They later watched the French revolution, where an elite ruling class, claiming to operate for the benefit of the working class, guillotined over 600,000 of its own people including priests, scholars, writers, Christians, and any who the ruling class felt were a threat to their power.

Our Founding Fathers knew that power corrupts and absolute power corrupts absolutely. Therefore, they created a federal government with limited powers. They divided the federal government into three branches (executive, legislative, and judicial) and defined the responsibilities and limits of each branch. They then limited the federal government's control to a very few specific areas. These included national defense, international treaties and trade, and security of the borders. The states were given the responsibility and power over all other areas not specifically specified.

Unfortunately, since the founding of the U.S. nation, the federal government politicians have slowly, deliberately, and methodically usurped power from the states and local communities. The attraction of ever-increasing power and control is intoxicating. It draws those in power to it like a moth to a beckoning light on a dark night. They can't control themselves and want to move closer and closer to the epicenter of power. There is a primal urge to gain absolute power over their world and everyone in their world. History is filled with stories of power-hungry dictators who wanted to control the entire world. Unfortunately, it doesn't turn out well for the rest of society when these powerful leaders and governments gain absolute control. Our Founding Fathers were trying to save us from the consequences.

It is time for the American people to push back on the ever growing power in Washington D.C. It is time to save the republic and restore the federal government back to its original concepts. It is time to undo the power concentration which has occurred over the past 200 years and at a much faster pace over the last 75 years. Programs created during the New Deal, Great Society, and Obamacare need to be dismantled at the federal level. They should be replaced with programs which are managed and controlled at the state or local level.

The American people are altruistic and desire to help the poor and disabled in this country. They have provided charity and support for their neighbors, families, and friends since before the U.S. became its own country. They have not needed help, direction, or interference from the federal government for most of that history. And they do not need help from the federal government now. What they need is for the federal government to get out of the way. People at the local levels of government can provide much better help to those in need, because those needing the help live within their communities. At the local level, the help can be provided faster and more targeted to the specific needs. There will also be much less chance of fraud and abuse. Since the local communities are aware of the opportunities in their specific areas, they can help people get back on their feet faster, thus reducing the charity needed. Most people, if they are able, prefer to work and be productive members of society rather than live off of charity.

There is a way which the federal government can help without managing and controlling the welfare programs. The federal government collects large amounts of revenue through taxes. A portion of these taxes could be set aside and provided back to the states in block grants, based on the needs of the states. The states, in turn, could then provide grants to their local communities based on their needs. The federal government's participation should be limited to collecting the funds and transferring those funds to the states and local governments.

There are many areas today where the federal government has created huge, expensive departments for controlling areas of the economy which are beyond their Constitutional authority. The responsibility for managing and controlling these areas need to be moved back to the state governments. If desired, the federal government can collect the taxes for funding these activities and provide block grant funds back to the states with no strings attached. It will be up to each state to then manage and control those areas.

CHAPTER 10:

CONCLUSION

For the first time in American history, the U.S. economy appears to be in major, long-term trouble. The federal government's debt is growing out-of-control with deficit spending forecast for as far as can be seen. Entitlement spending and interest on the debt are consuming all the federal revenue, leaving nothing to pay for current government programs. The total cost for operating the federal government each year is borrowed. Many states are also in financial trouble, needing to borrow to fulfill their obligations. The accruing liabilities for Medicare, Medicaid, Social Security, and government pensions are growing beyond the governments' ability to pay. Unemployment is running at levels not seen since the Great Depression and getting worse. The number of Americans classified at the poverty level is increasing, whereas the wealthy are increasing their wealth. Most jobs of

U.S. companies are being created in, or moved to, Asia, while jobs are being lost by the thousands within the U.S. It seems that there is nothing but bad news at present and few solutions are being offered.

This is the right time to rethink the policies and programs of the federal government. This is the right time to make changes which will get the federal government and the nation back on the right track. This is the right time to seriously evaluate the ideas presented in this book and decide if they make sense and will help. It is time to open our minds to new ideas. The time for the right kind of changes is NOW!!!

Chapter 1:

"List of amendments to the United States Constitution." <u>Wikipedia, The Free Encyclopedia</u>. Wikimedia Foundation, Inc. Sept. 30, 2011. <http://en.wikipedia.org/wiki/List_of_amendments_to_the_United_States_Constitution>

"U.S. Federal Individual Income Tax Rates History, 1913-2011 (Nominal and Inflation-Adjusted Brackets)." <u>Tax Foundation</u>. Sept. 9, 2011. <http://www.taxfoundation.org/publications/show/151.html>

"Distribution of Wealth." <u>Wikipedia, The Free Encyclopedia</u>. Wikimedia Foundation, Inc. Sept. 14, 2011. <http://en.wikipedia.org/wiki/Distribution_of_wealth>

Chapter 2:

"Social Security & Medicare Tax Rates." <u>Social Security Online</u>. December 29, 2010. <http://www.ssa.gov/OACT/ProgData/taxRates.html>

"FERS, Federal Employees Retirement System, An Overview of Your Benefits." <u>United States Office of Personnel Management</u>. April, 1998. <http://www.opm.gov/forms/pdfimage/RI90-1.pdf>

"Get salary and pension. Many government retirees also get public paychecks." <u>The Dispatch</u>, Moline, IL, Oct. 2, 2011: page 1.

"Union leaders pull down millions in pensions." The Dispatch, Moline, IL, Oct. 9, 2011, page 1.

Chapter 3:

"List of amendments to the United States Constitution." Wikipedia, The Free Encyclopedia. Wikimedia Foundation, Inc. Sept. 30, 2011. <http://en.wikipedia.org/wiki/List_of_amendments_to_the_United_States_Constitution>

"The Constitution of the United States." U.S. Constitution Online. March 6, 2011. <http://www.usconstitution.net/const.html>

"Judicial activism." Wikipedia, The Free Encyclopedia. Wikimedia Foundation, Inc. Sept. 23, 2011. <http://en.wikipedia.org/wiki/Judicial_activism>

Chapter 4:

"Physician advocacy." TMLT, Texas Medical Liability Trust. <http://www.tmlt.org/newscenter/physicianadvocacy.html>

"News release." Kaiser Family Foundation. Sept. 27, 2011. <http://www.kff.org/insurance/092311nr.cfm>

Chapter 5:

Riedl, Brian. "Federal Spending by the Numbers 2010." The Heritage Foundation. June 1, 2010. <http://www.heritage.org/Research/Reports/2010/06/Federal-Spending-by-the-Numbers-2010>

"Historical Tables. Table 1.1—Summary of Receipts, Outlays, and Surpluses or Deficits (-): 1789–2016." Office of Management and Budget. The White House. <http://www.whitehouse.gov/omb/budget/Historicals>

"Debt Clock Time Machine." U.S. Debt Clock. Org. <http://www.usdebtclock.org/>

"Historical Debt Outstanding - Annual 2000 – 2010." TreasuryDirect. Oct. 1, 2010. <http://www.treasurydirect.gov/govt/reports/pd/histdebt/histdebt_histo5.htm>

"2010 Census Data." U.S. Census Bureau. 2010. <http://2010.census.gov/2010census/data/>

Chapter 6:

Johnson, Chalmers. Nemesis: The Last Days of the American Republic. New York: Metropolitan, 2007

"List of United States military bases." Wikipedia, The Free Encyclopedia. Wikimedia Foundation,

Inc. Sept. 22, 2011. <http://en.wikipedia.org/wiki/List_of_United_States_military_bases>

"Military Funding - The U.S. Military Budget." MILITARYBASES.com. 2011. >http://militarybases.com/>

Chapter 7:

"United States Department of Education." Wikipedia, The Free Encyclopedia. Wikimedia Foundation, Inc. Sept. 29, 2011. <http://en.wikipedia.org/wiki/United_States_Department_of_Education>

"Fiscal Year 2012 Budget Summary — February 14, 2011." U.S. Department of Education. Feb. 14, 2011. <http://www2.ed.gov/about/overview/budget/budget12/summary/edlite-section1.html>

Chapter 9:

"What were Thomas Jefferson's view on a central government." WikiAnswers. Answers Corporation. 2011 <http://wiki.answers.com/Q/What_were_Thomas_Jefferson's_view_on_central_government>

"James Madison." Wikipedia, The Free Encyclopedia. Wikimedia Foundation, Inc. Sept. 28, 2011. <http://en.wikipedia.org/wiki/James_Madison>

"John Adams." <u>Wikipedia, The Free Encyclopedia</u>. Wikimedia Foundation, Inc. Sept. 23, 2011. <http://en.wikipedia.org/wiki/ John_Adams#Thoughts_on_Government>